Copyright © 2019 Tekkan
Artwork Copyright © 2019

All rights reserved.
First Printing, 2018
ISBN 978-1-7324107-8-7

To contact Tekkan please email:
buddhaboy1289@gmail.com

Table of Contents

Vietnam . . . . Page 92

How to Read My Poems

I have married the sonnet to the tanka. I tell a story in the sonnet — using three quatrains, separated by line spaces, and a final couplet. The story builds to a conclusion in the couplet. The tanka is a commentary, or a counterpoint, to the sonnet — the combined poems have two endings.

I don't rhyme my sonnets, because I want freer expression. I want to be direct in my meaning — I want people to clearly understand my meaning. The metaphors are inspired by Shakespeare, and the (aimed-for) precision is in imitation of Japanese style. Using the sonnet with the tanka, I am mixing the sensibility of the Occident and the Orient — which I have done by living in England, Japan, and America.

I don't punctuate much in my poetry. I want the words themselves to do the work. There is logic between words, and the forms provide structure. By not using punctuation I hope to direct readers to carefully attend to each word — to appreciate the graininess of words.

Reading my poems silently, say, on a bus, a train, or an airplane, and reading them aloud, may be different experiences. The way I've written there's not always a pause intended at the end of the line. Hint: *My poems are to be recited not as lines, but as phrases, and a phrase often overflows the break at the end of a line. I pause and take a breath where it seems natural for me to pause. Another person may pause differently than I do.*

Each single poem is a piece of a mosaic, and it is my hope that the collection of poems form an accurate portrait of consciousness.

My daughter, Jocelyn MacDonald, is a wonderful artist. Her art work graces this book.

I am Barry MacDonald. I received the *dharma* name, *Tekkan*, which means, Iron Man, a settled practitioner of great determination.

— *Tekkan*

Everyday Mind VIII

The sky was clear but
now there is a
downpour and a
splashing of puddles
on my driveway.

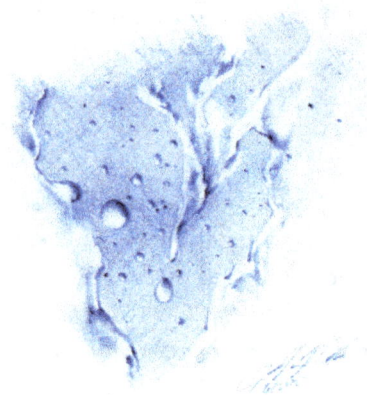

With the whoosh of the burner firing
I look up and see a hot air balloon
Floating in the air and it looks so odd
Suspended in the sky and there is the

Burst of flame and the rise of the balloon
And the gradual drifting and there are
The several balloons peopling the
Sky but the people are too far to see —

Only on the cloudless days of summer
Do balloons appear in such festive colors
And I imagine the buoyancy and
The view of the river on a sunny

Afternoon and there is no purpose for
The ride except for the effervescence.

What does the
valley look like with the sun
sparkling on the river
and reflecting off the windows
of the moving cars?

It is a human predicament that
We can't really live without relying
On some opinion about the after-
Life and the determination each of

Us makes is as much emotional as
Intellectual — and it's easier
To adopt a tradition and follow
A well-worn path — but I can't help thinking

One life cycle isn't enough because
Circumstances are limiting and I
Have my responses and outcomes that
Are only a morsel of what is

Possible — could I already be on
A journey of consecutive lifetimes?

The taste of life
is often bitter and
I seem compelled
to find a better
way to live.

The cottonwood outside my window is
Doomed because of a lightning strike from years
Ago that left a gash in the bark and
Exposed the core of the tree — and the tree

Has been leafing and filling the air with
Puffs as it should every year — and the view
From the window that inspires me in
The morning will never be the same — when

There was a white sky and snow on the ground
A pileated woodpecker appeared
And began to peck on the core of the
Cottonwood and I was enamored with

Its enormous size and with its crested
Red head but it was damaging the tree.

The arborist looked
at the exposed core and the
gaping holes and thought
such a gargantuan and
damaged tree was dangerous.

The cottonwood is doomed because of our
Decision to take it down before it falls
In a storm and damages the house and
The view from my window will be changed

Permanently which makes a difference
To me — for four years now every morning
I have come to my desk and window to
Capture something worth remembering and

Sometimes an event from yesterday comes
To mind but often when I am quiet
The most ordinary things emerge
In an extraordinary light and for

Years I have played with sunrises and light
And squirrels and birds and this cottonwood.

Through grade school
junior high school and
high school I didn't
notice this cottonwood tree
until I wrote poetry.

Each leaf of the cottonwood is taking
The sunlight and converting it to life
And energy and the tree is doing
Its part in effusing oxygen and

Thereby providing breathable air to
So many living beings but the tree
Experiences life differently
From me becoming responsive in spring

And frozen during the winter while I
Can marvel as the leaves are turning and
Sparkling in the light and I also
Appreciate its magnificence and

When the men with equipment come to take
It down that will be a very sad day.

The cottonwood was
present during my childhood
and when I returned
from living in
England and Japan.

My home is two blocks from my office and
My office is in the house where I grew
Up as I run the family business
That my Dad began fifty years ago

And it's remarkable that there are two
Towering cottonwoods in my life — one
Outside my window where I begin my
Morning by writing poetry and the

Other is on the corner of Martha
And Sycamore streets where my home is and
I have had to dispose of cottonwood
Leaves for over twenty years in the fall —

And I wonder how much different my
Life would be out from under cottonwoods.

When the wind is
moving cottonwood leaves
the breath of life
is audible
and visible.

I've worn glasses from my earliest years
And I am so used to seeing the world
Through gold rims and lenses that I never
Notice them anymore — and as I am

Sitting and standing and walking about
And lying down my arms and legs and hands
And feet are always visible but they
Are not the focus of my attention —

My body is a puppet and I am
The master pulling strings and behaving
As I please by showering dressing and
Eating — and I can get in a car and

Drive to a gathering of my friends and
Watch the other puppet masters playing.

A persisting
tooth ache is an
awakening — the pain
won't go unless I visit
a dentist.

The ownership of the hotel has changed
And all the managers who were there when
She started have moved on to better jobs
As this is chain of modestly priced

Hotels that doesn't pay employees well
But does fill with guests on the weekend — and
She has been named best employee of the
Month several times because she cleans each of

The rooms diligently and is cheerful
With the guests even when they are rude — and
Now every person who worked there when she
Began has left and she is loyal to

The guests and once in a while someone will
Recognize her worthiness with a tip.

She works
diligently
where others
just don't care.

The maintenance guy has quit — so there is
No one to fix the leaky faucet — and
The general manager used all the
Maternity leave she was entitled to

And then she quit — the typical sort of
Housekeepers can't be relied on to change
The bed sheets or scrub the toilets and they
Can't be depended on to show up for

Work — The hotel is down to a couple
Of front desk managers who do double
Shifts without assurance of relief — and
There are only several hardworking

Housekeepers cleaning and serving breakfast
And wondering — how long can this go on?

The hotel is booked
six months ahead and
looks like any other
establishment but the
management collapsed.

On a morning in July there are a
Few cottonwood puffs floating and there
Are two white insets flying sinuously
In a gloriously blue sky and they are

Chasing each other — and then I lose sight
Of them among the cottonwood leaves that
Are bright with sunlight — and the sun is an
Imposing white disk with a yellow fringe —

And I am happy to have attended
A meeting where we promulgated the
Importance of living in today and
Not yesterday or tomorrow because

We are never far from February
And shoveling snow in Minnesota.

As one among
sober alcoholics
it's good to
counteract
curmudgeoncy.

The deep grooves of the cottonwood bark are
Perfect for squirrels to clamber up — if
I were a squirrel the immensity
Of the cottonwood outside my window

Would be worth the exploration of a
Lifetime as there are pathways upwards to
A dizzy height that would be the end of
The world to a squirrel — and there is the

Temptation of the outward branches that
At the furthest extent dangle downwards
Challenging the courage of squirrels who
Have no reason to go there — I admire

The tenacity of compulsively
Climbing squirrels — don't they get exhausted?

Watching squirrels is
amusing and often
I don't really want
to turn my attention
to politics.

I don't know how to practice politics
And to associate with like-minded
Compatriots without also having
The suspicions and the bitterness that

We direct at people of opposing
Loyalties — because it seems that every
Organized political movement needs
Heroes and ideals that are worthy

Of sacrifice — and a party needs its
Oppressors and outrages against whom
Action is necessary — the drive for
Conquest makes a virtue of deception

And it takes honesty and compassion
To have opponents but not enemies.

History
is heroic
demonizing
romantic and
intoxicating.

I didn't feel the heat of the morning
Until the little black fly with green eyes
Landed on my arm and walked about with
Little legs over the fine hair on my

Arm — and I discovered not wanting to
Expend the energy necessary
To flick it away so I just watched it
Instead and noticed the slightest tickle —

And a little while later a tiny
Black ant proceeded to explore my arm
Too and I noticed the tickle again —
And the ants and the flies have as much right

As I do to enjoy the summer air
But I won't give the mosquitoes a pass.

As the air becomes
hotter even in the shade
of a tree I start
to feel a little dizzy
and warmer inside and out.

Kit Cat is drawn to the windows of our
Home and we have determined that he and
Johnnie and Henry are house cats to be
Fed regularly and freed from hunting

And killing — and it is a little sad
To hear Kit Cat whining at the window
And see him sniffing a summer breeze with
His ears forward and with his eyes focused

On something outside — and he is hunched and
Poised as if to pounce — but of course he can't —
And on the occasions when I step out
Without being careful and he escapes

He runs and hops — and he rolls in the dirt
And chews the grass — and he lets me catch him.

Kit is delicate
maneuvering among the
cans and packages
on the kitchen counter — front
paws precise — back following.

There are afternoons when I leave all of
The car windows open to feel the breeze
Blowing through and other days when it is
Better to use the air conditioner

When there is a moist and sticky feeling
About the heat — and in the middle of
July wind continues to toss the limbs
And leaves of the trees but the motion and

The sound aren't as noticeable to
Me as the heat and the sun are much more
Prominent but when I see the long leaves
Of a willow flowing within a breeze

All the elements I love about the
Summer are included with the willow.

There is fluid grace
about the long willow leaves
in a summer breeze
as the sun the wind and the
willow are in harmony.

I am now over sixty years old but
That has very little to do with my
Behavior because I go to the gym
And am especially spry and put the

Younger guys to shame in comparison
But it's been pointed out to me when I
Bend over to tie my shoe or when I
Rise from my chair at the coffee shop a

Groan will often escape from me — but I
Am not complaining because I wouldn't
Know I was doing it if the people
Nearby weren't informing me — anyway

I do remember long ago others
Letting me know that I was grimacing.

I am not in charge
of what my body does —
beyond the choosing
of the activity and
the energy expended.

I was walking with a friend who enjoys
Gardening and asked about a shrubby
Plant with tiny purple blossoms that we
Were passing by — because I was seeing

The plant everywhere while driving about
Stillwater and it was just another
Thing I didn't know — like the names of the
Different kinds of wildflowers — and she

Said it is a Russian Sage and that it
Blooms in July and August — and it's not
Important — like following the daily
News is — as it is just a happening

So easy to overlook — but now I
Am wondering does it come from Russia?

At the coffee shop
we discovered from the
Internet that it
is eatable and it is
useful for relieving pain.

It was Saturday afternoon with a
Week of bother behind me — and I was
Done with most of my chores for the day and
Didn't want to do anything extra

And because I had no plans and it would
Have taken effort to reach someone who
Probably would already be busy
By then I decided to take a nap —

Because the sunny linen on my bed
Was inviting — and I stretched out in a
Separation from consciousness — and when
I awoke the bottom of my left foot

Was cozy and I became aware of
Something furry — Kit Cat was joining me.

The nap was a
hole in a sunny
afternoon — and
then I went shopping
for groceries.

On Twitter people are allowed to type
Two hundred eighty letters including
Punctuation in the composition
Of a message that they can transmit on

The Internet — and there are millions of
People communicating messages
And a celebrity will acquire
Millions of followers who happily

Have access to a famous person's thoughts —
But the medium devolved into a
Method for exchanging insults and for
Empowering groups of enraged people

Who enforce politically correct speech
By attacking in a virtual mob.

People have taken
an empty form capable
of concise beauty
but they are cultivating
hostility.

Meeting a friend for conversation in
Downtown Stillwater and sitting on a
Bench by the river before the town is
Open for business in the morning is

The epitome of luxury as
The air is chilly but warming — and the
Sun is reflecting off the water in
Flecks of gold — and in the distance there is

The high span of the St. Croix Crossing Bridge
Stretching across the valley in graceful
Lines — and there are the several ornate
Riverboats with paddlewheels that are docked

Nearby — and we have the freedom to say
Anything curious or trivial.

An open sky is
reflective of boundless
possibility —
conversation often
prompts discovery.

I am not the center of anyone's
Attention except of my own and a
Hobby — like connecting isolated
Words — is helpful for lifting my center

Of gravity — because I know thinking
About disrespect or discourtesy
Or a lack of appreciation makes
Thinking in a lighter mood just about

Impossible — if I am relying
On a divine something at work in the
Way things are then I need to cultivate
The faith that the divine is not apart

From the problem I can not evade but
The divine is a part of the problem.

I can't solve all my
problems by playing
with words but by
playing with words
I am happier.

I may be unsophisticated and
Unfamiliar with the conceptions of
Scientific classification but
If there are three dimensions — up and down —

Left and right — forward and backward — along
With a fourth dimension of time why can't
We consider life that somehow emerged
From the material of particles

And molecules as a fifth dimension
And why can't we assign consciousness that
Supersedes the purposeful functioning of
A heart arteries and capillaries

As a sixth dimension including a
Spectrum of rhinoceros and human?

A spirit moves
choosing direction
and velocity
surrounded by
other spirits.

By the time Friday afternoon comes most
Of the oomph of the workweek escapes me
And the dissipation of energy
And focus is not intentional but

Is just a matter of habit — and on
Saturday morning I can wake an hour
Later and be liberated from the
Pressure of earning money — and the day

Has a touch of a holiday about
It that often extends into Sunday
Morning and afternoon — but once the dishes
On Sunday evening are washed an air

Of seriousness settles upon me
As I think about what I need to do.

As a conscious
tomato I would know
the sun and night
the heat and chill
and bug feet.

There is a video on Facebook of a
Couple of kids after a down pouring
Of rain who have goggles for swimming and
And a bicycle and some muddy ground

And one of them gets on the bike and grips
The brakes and the other kneels behind the
Back tire and while wearing the goggles with
Much joyful expectation he says "go"

And he is covered by a spattering
Of mud — which is an improvement of the
Jackson Pollack style — because Jackson was
Dripping paint on canvas by himself and

Jackson never did escape depression
But the boys together were jubilant.

Eventually
sophistication
spoils
spontaneity.

Stillwater doesn't have the Zen Temples
Kyoto has and doesn't have the Shinto
Shrines and the imperial palaces
Or the stone lanterns and tori gates

And in Stillwater we don't hear bamboo
Knocking together in a breeze and we
Don't have the rising and fading throb of
Cicadas that permeates the summer

But there is a majestic river in
Stillwater wider than the Kamo in
Kyoto and there are the limestone bluffs and
The historic courthouse with a cannon

And in summer there are humming birds and
Swallows and many kinds of wildflowers.

There is a mountain
in Kyoto where monkeys
live but in Stillwater
there are butterflies
and dragonflies.

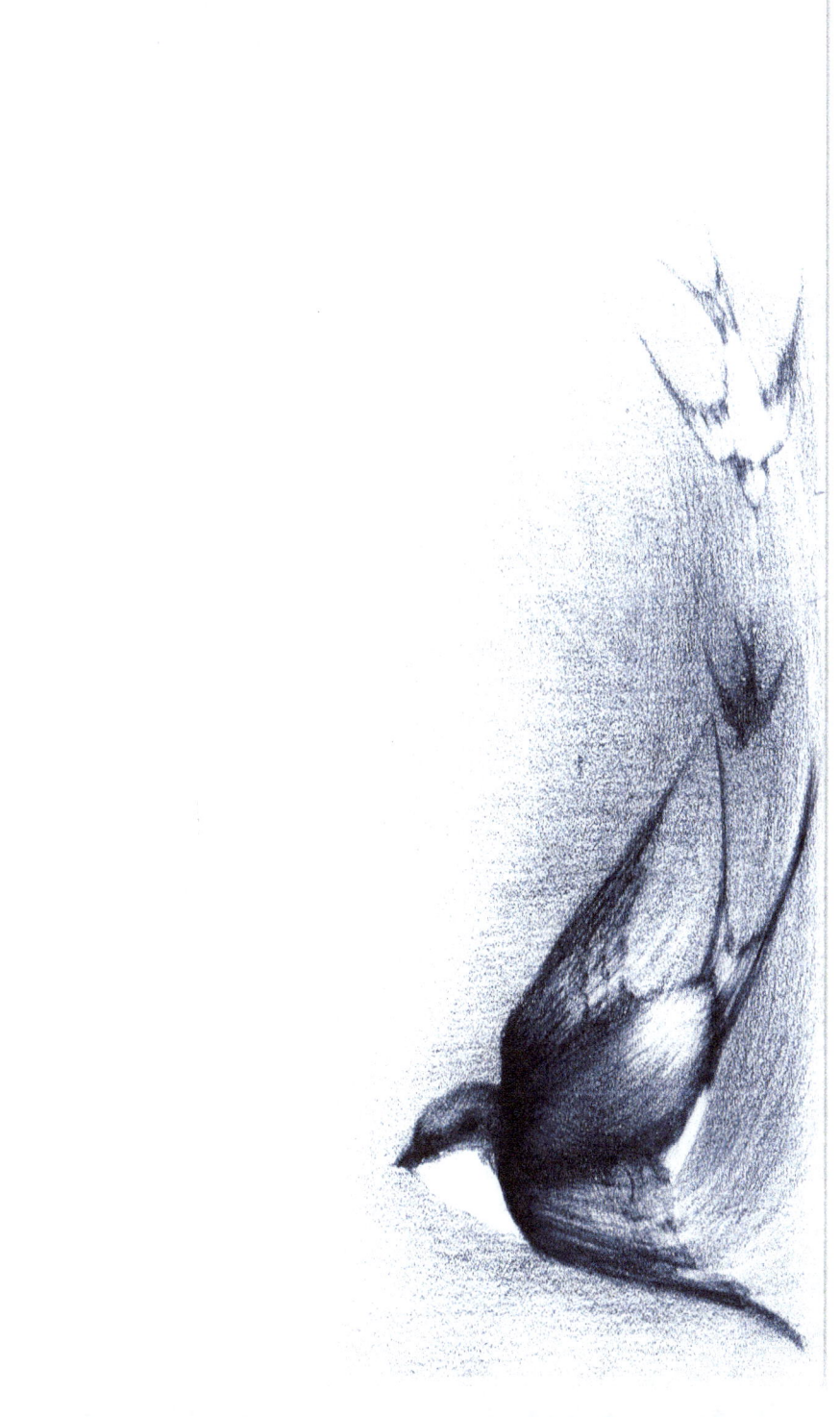

Kyoto and has a golden temple in the
North and a silver temple in the east
And there is a Zen rock garden where the
Monks rake the tiny pebbles sashaying

A harmonious pattern — and if you
See the traditional tile roofs of the
Temples and the homes you will not forget
The stylized mixture of pine trees and

Tiles — but there are also buildings made
Of concrete slabs that are stained by sticky
Smog along side the garish neon of
Pachinko Parlors where the Japanese

Play pinball while chain-smoking cigarettes
And staring with zombie fascination.

On television
Americans relive
cowboy shootouts and
Japanese cavort with
samurai slashings.

I embody and cherish the months when
I left my guest home in Yamashina
In the morning and walked over a ridge
Of mountains on the east side of Kyoto

For my destination downtown where I
Taught English in a language school and on
The way I passed bamboo and pine and the
Pagoda of the Kyomizu Temple

And the vermillion Ya Saka Shrine and
The Geisha district and the Kabuki
Theater — and I remember throbbing
Cicadas and the summer haze and the

Worn and secluded footpath and the view
Of Kyoto surrounded by the mountains.

I am following
Japanese masters
on their footpaths
collecting insights
for poetry.

I love peaches and am big fan of
The fuzz on the red and yellow skin and
When eating only a peach I close my
Eyes and think "I really do love peaches"

And usually it's my habit to
Slice a peach into sections and sometimes
I prefer thick slices and sometimes thin
But every morning is good with peaches

And blueberries and granola and milk
And my tongue will taste the blueberry and
My teeth will crunch the granola and the
Milk provides the slushy harmony that

Fills my mouth with goodness but it is the
Piquancy of the peach that is joyful.

I close my eyes
and can't stop
dreaming of peaches.

Blood Moon

In North America we weren't able
To see the lunar eclipse in July
That was the longest eclipse of the moon
By the earth in this century — but the

People in Africa the Middle East
And in Asia could have seen it if they
Had the inclination to watch sunlight
Passing through the atmosphere of the earth

And bending around the earth to fall on
The moon — and the watchers who know the facts
Would understand the air of the earth was
Scattering the shorter waves of blue and

Green and letting the longer waves at the
Redder end of the spectrum continue.

We comprehend so
many more facts about the
way things are without
satisfying the push
of our curiosity.

As it happens the astronauts who walked
About the moon came back with hay fever
With watery eyes and sore throats and the
Dust was clinging to their suits and clogging

Equipment and filling the craft with the
Smell of burnt gunpowder — the particles
Were fifty times as small as the width of
A human hair — and they are as sharp as

Glass — and because gravity is so much
Weaker on the moon when the astronauts
Moved in their land rovers they raised a cloud
Of dust that lingered around and because

There is no atmosphere the dust of the
Moon is electro-statically charged.

Fanciful stories
about the moon being made
of green cheese turn out
to be imaginative
nonsensical palaver.

When listening to the scientists their
Knowledge and their desire to conquer
Ignorance is obvious — and I have
The impression their wonderment about

The facts of the universe is burdened
With the fearsome immensity and the
Hostility to life that the cosmos
Reveals — moon dust is inhospitable

To breathing lungs — and some scientists do
Ascribe randomness to the way things are
That drains away any meaning any
Person would like to find in the events

Of life — to which I answer that life and
Consciousness are undeniable facts.

We cannot capture
and pin the butterfly of
divinity to
a board where everyone can
grasp its entire meaning.

Usually the alarm wakes me from
A dream and I am groggy — and my first
Sensation is the yowling of Johnnie
For his cat food — and I charge my cell phone

And tablet and make the bed and change my
Clothes and puff on the inhaler — that makes
Me rinse my mouth — and I squirt medicine
Inside of Henry the cat to treat his

Kidney disease and sometimes I may be
Distracted by an email while Johnnie
Is getting noisier and is yowling
Insistently because he is hungry

And wants his food while I appear to be
Quite unresponsive and indifferent.

On some days it takes
more time to get to Johnnie
and I must appear
a cruel and a capricious
kind of deity to him.

When I know what to look for I see it —
Almost as if the thing I was looking
For was waiting for me — but there is a
Side effect of having expectations

That by narrowing my focus I see
Less than I could otherwise — and I was
Driving around Stillwater on the third
Of August and there was a red leaf at

The top of a tree where I saw a red
Leaf last year that was a hint of autumn
Coming — and even though summer seems like
An established fact and winter seems an

Impossibility the sight of a
Scarlet leaf reminds me of transitions.

I also saw a
little yellow butterfly
flitting in a breeze
in its peculiar fashion
living a butterfly life.

I saw Kit Cat lounging on the window
Sill of my bedroom and he was absorbed
With the outside while I was making my
Way to the car to drive away and then

Quick like the devil he followed me out
The door and cavorted — and yesterday
After I gave him a dish of food that
Usually consumes his attention

I opened the door and reached for the mail
In the box and out scooted Kit Cat in
A snap — and then he cavorted — so I
Realize alertness is paramount

Because he may seem to be busy but
He is always conniving to escape.

His brain is the
size of a golf ball
and yet he is
making a monkey
of me.

We meditate in a little chapel
Inside a church for twenty minutes and
The Doan rings the bell and we stand up
And file out of the room on the way to

The sanctuary where we walk in steps
Of silent meditation for fifteen
Minutes — and we return to the chapel

For sitting meditation — the Doan
Stands by the door as we file in — and this
Morning after the first sitting I was
The last in line and I snatched the bell and

Carried it and on reentering the
Chapel I returned it to the Doan.

The confusion
and astonishment
in the middle of
the quiet was quite
satisfying.

We were putting the chapel in order
After we finished meditating by
Stacking the mats and cushions and
By returning the chairs to their places

Inside the chapel — after taking them
Out beforehand — and we were enjoying
Conversation in the vestibule as
We always do — and I was partaking

Of the meditative afterglow and
The clarity and reached in my pocket
For my keys — but they were not there — and I
Felt in my other pocket with no luck

Did I leave my keys in the ignition?
And did I lock myself out of the car?

I rushed on the
sidewalk expected the
worst but I noticed
the car keys were hidden
in my hand.

It's been discovered that the vacuum of
Space is not empty even though nothing
Is there — because in quantum space packets
Of energy are winking in and out

Of time — and no one knows where these tiny
Particles are coming from — and so the
Void of the cosmos is permeated
With an enormous quantity of what

Is believed virtual energy — and
I am wondering whether the thoughts I
Will have this afternoon that I have no
Conception of now will come from the same

Mysterious nowhere that the quanta
Come from — from a virtual consciousness.

Once in a while I
would appreciate
variety so
I could overcome the
drag of my habits.

The eye of science is relentless and
Scientists have found waves of gravity
And are postulating a gravity
Particle and they have discovered a

Particle that provides elements with
Mass they call the Higgs Boson that comes from
The Higgs Field — so I speculate — are they
Looking for the particle imparting

Consciousness — and if not why not — because
Consciousness is a reality and
We should have explanations to oppose
The randomality that drains meaning

From existence — because it would be good
To discover meaning in the cosmos.

If someday a
consciousness particle
is discovered I'd
suggest a name —
the Barry particle.

I imagine myself a simpleton
Moving about but only aware of
Two dimensions — forwards and backwards — and
Side to side — and if a sphere were imposed

About me — not being aware of up
And down — I could not incorporate the
Reality of the sphere extending
Above and below me — but I am not

A simpleton and I can understand
The third dimension of height and the fourth
Dimension of time and I can read what
Scientists write and can admire how

Far they are extending the boundaries
To what we can possibly understand.

Perhaps
a black hole is
an event involving
nine or eleven
dimensions?

A crew of five arrived in the morning
And they positioned a lift behind the
House near the cottonwood — and a man in
The lift cuts the tree with a chain saw — and

They placed a truck with a crane in front of
The house — and the guy in the lift attaches
The branches he cuts into cords the crane
Uses to raise the branches over the

House and onto the driveway — where the crew
Saws the branches into sections that the
Crane lifts into the trucks that will haul the
Cottonwood away — and I am watching

Through the window as the majestic trunk
Is standing but only for a moment.

Sawdust is
descending and an
open sky is replacing
a presence I've known
from childhood.

The cottonwood presented more heft than
The crew anticipated so a good
Length of the trunk remains this morning with
The familiar fork extending into

The sky and there is the clefting of the
Bark the two lightning strikes made and the holes
The woodpeckers left — and the largest hole
Was one of the reasons we decided

To take the tree down — but the branches and
The leaves are gone and I am facing the
Glare of the sun for the first morning with
An altered sense of normalcy and an

Appreciation for the heat of the
Sun that was filtered by cottonwood leaves.

In a week the crew
will return to take
the remaining trunk
with a machine to
grind up the stump.

The window serves as an extension of
My morning vision when I sit at my
Desk and formulate my thoughts about what
Is worthy of remembering today

And after surfing the Internet the
More than sixty people who were shot in
Chicago on the weekend and the blind
Eye the news media is turning to

The continuing catastrophe of
Violence and mismanagement of our
Largest cities demands attention but
The politicians and commentators

Would much rather talk about palaver
Personality and peccadilloes.

Everyday I looked
past the cottonwood seeing
neglect and bitterness
and I'm trying to be
optimistic.

There is a greyhound in this poem that
Is beautifully flexing and looks to be
Doing exactly what it is designed
For and it doesn't matter that the race

Is for show and that the mechanical
Rabbit is a contrivance to spur the
Hound to expend itself and it is not
Significant that there are other dogs

Competing alongside because I am
Watching this greyhound be a greyhound just
Like music is music and full of joy
And the race will be over soon enough

But it is only in the doing of
Life that things are properly realized.

The resting
afterwards is an
occasion for
reflection and
appreciation.

On a Sunday I was enjoying the
Southward view of the winding valley from
The elevated bluff of Pioneer
Park — I resolved to walk to the St. Croix

Crossing bridge far in the distance to the
South and I wanted to cross the span that
Was high above the river — to measure
The distance there and back with my feet — and

To see the river rippling below
The bridge — and I was curious about
The new walkway from Stillwater to the
Bridge — because there are many things I have

Never seen — and there were white butterflies
And I met a friend on a bicycle.

In about four
hours I returned to
the cherry tree in
Pioneer Park —
footsore.

The pulsation of waves coming in to
The shore as I was walking to the bridge
Was quicker than I supposed waves to be —
Then I remembered this is a river

And the waves were the result of a wake
From one of the boats on the river so
These were man-made emanations flowing
On the surface — and down the bank and through

The trees I could hear and glimpse the sight of
A jet skier bouncing on the water
And I imagined the freedom to leave
For anywhere on a whim and arrive

In a snap — but to me the jet skier
Was irritating like a mosquito.

The whine and the
impudence of the
coming and going
makes me a little
envious.

It was a little triumph to make it
To the bridge because it took more than an
Hour to arrive — but I considered
The walk a holiday because it was

Outside of my routine — and as I was
Ascending to a great height I saw the
Tallest cottonwoods by the shore below
Me — and the avenue of the bridge in

The sky seemed like a grand destination
With a walk-way for pedestrians and
With plaques at intervals explaining the
History of the frontier and of the

Watershed — of the nesting of eagles
And of the migration of tanagers.

I was rewarded
For years of
observation —
the new bridge
transformed the valley.

After resisting pressure to conform
To what everyone else is doing I
Joined Facebook — because I want to share my
Poems and sell books — and I entered the

Cyber world that is a carnival — with
Videos of performing animals
Photos of far away places and I
Reconnected with people I forgot

And I chatted with people in Bhutan
India and the Philippines and in
New Guinea — and I am barraged with friend
Requests from young women who are busting

Out of their clothes — who if they were here would
Probably not behave as they appear.

Out of touch
and far away —
what do these
women want?

I was driving and parked my car when my
Phone rang with an unusual jingle —
And I said hello and heard an Asian
Woman who I could not understand and

I heard a commotion that was hard to
Interpret but apparently there were
Two women conversing like birds and I
Think they are Chinese — they were giggling

And were waiting for a response from me
And I lowered the phone from my ear and
Saw two beautiful young women looking
At me because somehow they triggered the

Video capacity I never
Use — we blinked together and they vanished.

It was a summons
and a dismissal out of
the blue of Facebook
endlessly fascinating
and signifying nothing.

I have only been on Facebook for a
Few days and have no idea what the
Common experience is — my purpose
Is to promote books of poetry to

As large a potential readership as
Possible and I have found most of my
Friend requests come from adorable young
Women who are struggling to stay in

Their clothes — and I have more than five thousand
Such friends — but I don't if know the women
Are really women and if they really
Are beautiful or if they are sweaty

Guys in Pittsburg with schemes to extract as
As much money from me as possible.

I am a cyber
version of a Hollywood
celebrity with a
constant barrage of grasping
from people I don't know.

I imagine who I'm chatting with — and
There is only a photo to go
By — and it's not so easy — because my
Finger is blunt and it has to be placed

Exactly on the screen of my phone that
Doesn't leave room for error — but I am
Touching a person in cyber space with
Every tap of my finger and I will

Not tell a lie because one lie will have
To be followed by another and the
Terrible distortion of lying would
Effect my face to face behavior too

So I will pay attention to what moves
Me — and let my fingers play with the words.

Cyber space is a
window to the unbounded
imagination —
I have to be poised within
myself to be healthy.

There is sawdust covering the grass and
The hill — and there is a massive stump that
Is all that is left of the cottonwood —
And I won't see the craggy bark that was

The playground of squirrels — and there will be
No more sprays of seeds in the spring — and I
Won't be able to imagine that the
Turning leaves in a wind up and down the

Height of the tree are bells anymore — and
I will not measure the buoyancy of
The air by watching the floating of the
Cottonwood puffs in June either — but now

I will have to wear a wide brimmed hat at
My desk as a shield from the sunny glare.

I don't know why the
guy said they would grind
out the stump at no
additional cost —
they didn't grind it.

My thoughts and emotions resemble a
Magic fountain constantly arising
And on some days an event will turn the
Direction of my thinking — and sometimes

In idleness I do return to a
Habitual flow of thoughts that may be
Oppressive and punishing of myself —
And when I am sad it is helpful to

Be forgiving and gentle with myself
Because I cannot wrench myself into
A better way of thinking — but if there
Is the practice of kindness the fountain

Will again produce enthusiasm
As negativity does dissipate.

Enthusiasm is
natural — practice
letting negativity
dissipate with
kindness.

When I was taking the offerings from
The cat box out to the trash container
Kit escaped again — because I forgot
That he watches my every move — and in

The darkness about dawn I could barely
See him scampering with his tail in the
Air because Kit Cat is brown and blends with
Shadows — but I hurried and I suspect

He wants to be caught because he's afraid
Of the outdoors and he runs to make me
Chase and I always do catch him — which I
Couldn't do if he wanted his freedom —

When I march back home with him dangling
Limply in my hands he's not struggling.

The dark at that time
of my morning routine
impressed itself on
me — night is growing wings and
winter is coming again.

I had an important business meeting
And was nervous and in a hurry and
I got mail and left the post office and
To avoid a slowpoke in front of me

I looked in my rearview mirror and saw
Nothing so I turned the steering wheel right
And backed up and — smacked into a parked car —
I jumped out and there was damage on the

Driver's door and a big dent on my rear
Bumper — I didn't see anyone and
I could have left — my fourth accident in
Four years — oh my God — my insurance will

Triple quadruple — and I thought if I
Drove away now could I really escape?

I trudged next door
to the police station
to have a report made
and I met a beautiful
police woman.

Driving home last night with the windows of
The car open I heard the throbbing of
The crickets giving the air texture — this
Morning while I was meditating with

The windows open I noted that the
Darkness was creeping earlier into
The morning — and I heard a gentle rain
Hitting the roof and I noticed how the

Water sounds as it was running along
The gutters — there were little fears about
Attending to emails and changing the
Name and address on a checking account —

I lingered over a guy who is more than
An acquaintance and who is not a friend.

And then the impact
of the rain was fainter
and the light was
revealing the contents
of the room.

There is a little dot of green light that
Appears within the profile photo of
A person who uses the Messenger
App — and when the green dot is visible

The person is available to chat
At the moment — so if I want to talk
To Marilyn in the Philippines I
Type a message into a box on the

Screen and touch a pair of blue wings and my
Words are sent at the speed of light around
The Earth — Marilyn is having trouble
Falling asleep at night while the sun is

Rising here and something is bothering
Her but it's difficult to decipher.

There are glimmers
of personality
emotion and
an urge to control
in the use of words.

I was in the habit of coming to
My desk and window to watch the sunrise
And write poetry — but I joined Facebook
And accepted the friend requests of five

Thousand women with luscious photos — and
My phone buzzes with notifications
Of women from everywhere who want to
Chat with me from morning to night — and I

Juggle three conversations at once and
Fumble my typing and exchange photos
And chat face to face by video and
This new activity is distracting —

I am whirling in a cyber vortex
And am overlooking the sun and leaves.

I am a lonely
guy consuming
cotton candy
cyber
relationships.

I would love to go on vacation to
See the earth's highest tide at the Bay of
Fundy in Canada where the pull of
The moon on the ocean coming in and

Going out changes the depth of the sea
Over fifty feet — but I don't have the
Money or the time for a vacation —
So I will take the opportunity

In the spare moments of the day to look
For the little happenings about me
That I have never noticed before and
I will open my ears to the words of

My friends and savor the insights and the
Expressions coming with conversation.

I do not have to
go distances to
see the everyday
transformation of
this vivid moment.

A friend told me of an operation
Her mother is recovering from in
The hospital with the doctors and the
Nurses considering and balancing

The chemicals she needs — and the pace of
Her heart is monitored so that when she
Feels uncomfortable she can push a
Button and caretakers are alerted

At another location and they can
Adjust the flow of electrons needed
To stabilize the beating of her heart —
And her mother is disoriented

And wondering whether she has become
A machine dependant on technicians.

My friend said her
mother suffers because
her heart reflects the
burdens of people
in her life.

Facebook triggers my impulsivity
When I am driven to post my newest
Creation and don't want to take the time
To return to the poem in a few

Days to see whether I omitted words
Or could have made a more cogent point — and
After posting I become impatient
Returning to Facebook repeatedly

Throughout the day to see who has liked or
Commented on my poem as if I
Were seeking validation for myself —
And I am seeking for worthiness in

The ephemera of cyberspace — like
A teenager without experience.

Days or weeks later
someone I have never met
will comment on a
poem with unexpected
welcome reverberation.

There is rain without wind this morning and
The drumming of the rain through the windows
Punctuated my meditation and
The rain on the roof was tranquilizing

And now I am at my desk and looking
Out my window watching the rain descend
In a shower of tiny streaks that are
Only visible because of the green

Foliage of the trees — and I can see that
The gray sky the rain is falling from is
Glowing with a white light that reminds me
Even on a rainy day the sun is

Radiant — no matter what my troubles
Are simple observation is joyful.

The muggy heat of
last evening gave no hint
of the coolness and
the musical drops coming
and my bed sheets were sticky.

The I.R.S. became confused about
The name of my tax-exempt foundation
And the name of my magazine that is
Published by my tax-exempt foundation

Because my secretary used the wrong
Name on my paychecks — and my accountant
Sent a letter to the I.R.S. to
Alleviate the confusion and he

Said I had done nothing wrong and taxes
Were not owed — contrary to the claims of
Of the anonymous agents at the
I.R.S. — but I received a letter

Explaining that if I don't pay promptly
The agency will seize my property.

On this Labor Day
holiday weekend I am
thinking our letters
crossed in the mail and I am
determined not to worry.

The tallest waterfall on earth is called
The Angel Falls — it falls from a mountain range
In a South American jungle and
I will never see it except via

Video — but I can imagine the
River rushing between the rugged grey
Boulders and the water falling at the
Top into a quiet expanse of space

And I can see the dispersing droplets
Forming a mist subject to the wind and
I can appreciate the refraction
Of sunlight into a misty rainbow

And I can hear the impact of water
On water — a continuing marvel.

The falls were named after
Jimmy Angel whose puny
plane got stuck in the mud
on the mountain top — he
walked for eleven days
to find help.

I am lonely although usually
There is activity helping me to
Forget the fact of the loneliness — and
It is a thread of a woven garment

I am wearing in this lifetime — and while
There is much conversation and there are
Many companions to help me pass the
Time I am aware there is an absence

Where something needs to be — and I know how
To recognize the everyday trials and
Triumphs that are meaningful and I am
Able to generate the compassion

And the self-forgetting that could be love —
But something I don't know what is missing.

I am waiting
somehow to
articulate
and to absorb
intimacy.

He called this morning for the first time in
Over a year and we talked about the
Circles we go to that inspire our
Sobriety and enable us to

Turn around the negative attitudes
That can be dangerous — I spoke about
A similar gathering of people
Who address the afflictions of those who

Are related to alcoholics and
How it takes knowledgeable and focused
Effort to unlearn the coping skills of
Living with alcoholism as a

Child — and it is funny how a childhood
Interpretation does need correcting.

A child interprets
the craziness and neglect
of drunken parents
as justified punishment
for unlovable children.

I typed that she would be better off with
A younger guy nearby her — and I let
Go of her and went about my business —
But twenty minutes later my phone buzzed

And looking at my phone in my hand I
Saw her looking at me — and she is a
Beauty and knows that she is beautiful
And she is intelligent and crafty

With technology — her audacity
Was captivating and I was spellbound —
Many things are always happening at
The same time and there was an impact in

Our meeting face to face so suddenly —
Did I glimpse a vulnerability?

There can be such play
in the trading of words and
photos and video
and such anticipation —
what will I discover next?

The absence of the cottonwood outside
My window has continuing impact
As the cottonwood did so dominate
The view while I was putting my thoughts in

Order — and it was only on the odd
Day that the tree with craggy bark or the
Squirrels about the tree were the focus
Of my attention — but the tree was a

Fixture in the normalcy of life and
Now I am adjusting to the fact with
Fresh eyes — and a larger expanse of the
Sky is visible and the rising sun

Is more prominent and imposing and
Now the contrails of a jet are drifting.

The impact of
change is felt
suddenly and
gradually.

My friend who inherited a small farm
Told me of the differences from when
His father plowed with a team of horses —
The Department of Agriculture has

Mapped the taxability of every
Acre by using satellite data —
And the plowing and the harvesting are
Regulated by the government — and

Because corn is a world commodity
A farmer tending a small acreage
Is attentive to the tariffs between
America and China — and with the

Use of genetically modified
Crops lawsuits are disrupting the market.

Independence and
determination and brawn
aren't sufficient
anymore to operate
a cornfield in Iowa.

It takes a little exploration to
Realize most of the girls chatting on
Line over distances that make touching
Impossible are enticing men through

Words and photos and videos to give
Away their money — because so many
Are in the habit of chatting and are
So ingenious at attaching hooks

Into the psyche of men there must be
A mournful ocean of loneliness and
Addiction in cyberspace — though I know
How addiction deepens the loneliness

I did a little exploration but
I can't throw myself away so cheaply.

But Marilyn in
the Philippines
is genuinely
beautiful and
sweet.

From the view of Pioneer Park on a
Limestone bluff I could see the graceful lines
Of the St. Croix Crossing Bridge appearing
Tiny in the distance — and because it

Was a sunny Sunday and I was free
Of chores I decided to walk downtown
Stillwater and follow a walking path
By the river among the cottonwoods —

And on the way I took photos with my
Phone of the Lift Bridge in Stillwater with
The Crossing Bridge getting closer — and I
Sent the photos through the air to a girl

In Georgia and to another in the
Philippines to share in my adventure.

I ascended from
the riverbank and walked in
the sunlight towards the
gargantuan Crossing Bridge
anticipating marvels.

Starting out on the walking way over
The bridge the tallest cottonwoods on the
River bank were below me — and a mile
Ahead of me on the other side of

The bridge the people walking looked tiny
And as I was walking over the span
That crosses the valley and river at
A great height I listened to the cars and

Trucks and motorcycles passing in both
Directions and I noticed the waves of
Sound rose to a crescendo coming to
Me and diminished going away — and

The sound of traffic nearby or in the
Distance makes me feel a little lonely.

People move
together separately
continuously
transporting
solitary lives.

The sights and sounds on a day of walking
Are part of the event — and there is the
Exploration of hopes and desires
Or the reckless exercise of complaints

But the pleasure of walking for me is
The liberation of consciousness and
The discovery of meaning — and the
Words of Cid Corman returned to me from

Thirty years ago — and he said I should
Live my poetry — and maybe he meant
I should be sincere and generous and
That my words would be a reflection of

My spirit or perhaps he meant something
Else — but I do aim for sincerity.

Returning from the
Crossing Bridge striding the last
slope with aching feet
I felt the mild declining
sun with satisfaction.

The light on the leaves in the morning is
Golden in September and the air is
Crisp and if there were a time within the
Seasons that I would like to extend it

Would be September because the sun is
Not glaring and the afternoon heat is
Gentle — there are a few trees in town that
Are turning yellow and red but green is

Predominate and throughout the day when
A breeze is in the trees the light on the
Turning leaves is golden — that serves as a
Signal that now is the culmination

Of growth and a harvest is approaching
And then the days will become desolate.

I remember how
wind tosses leaves
in spring — there is a
boisterous joy.

The season for roses has passed this year
But when thinking about you roses come
To mind — because you are blooming in the
Sunny springtime of your life and you do

Approximate the velvet folds within
Folds that constitute a rose — and the moon
Has a mysterious allure because
Of its various shapes and colors and

Its movements — and the sun is marvelous
Because it is the resplendent source of
Breath and life — but you as you are now are
The epitome of beauty and love

Forcefully drawing me to you as if
I were under a spell and mesmerized.

Passion for
possession
is consuming
and thorns are
a warning.

The cherry in September is just such
A humble little tree surrounded by
The taller and broader trees reaching up
And out spreading their leaves — taking so much

More sunlight — and here is the maple in
Pioneer Park beginning to show the
Touches of orange that will become so
Brilliant in October — and Pioneer

Park is just a tiny area of
Stillwater on a bluff overlooking
The valley with a southward view of the
Turning river with the Crossing Bridge in

The distance — and Stillwater is just a
Modest town in a boisterous nation.

But when the cherry
is blooming in spring
its beauty is just
unsurpassable.

Of the unnumbered things I could have seen
On my walk from home over the Crossing
Bridge and back again I saw a yellow
Bird hopping among branches — and by the

River the wind was visible when a
Hawk was gliding and circling — and the
Broad surface of the water between the
Banks was undulating separately

From the current and bobbing a tied barge —
And from the view at the height of the bridge
Shadows of clouds were moving on the trees
On both sides of the river — and on the

Way back under the cottonwoods I heard
A cricket punctuate the afternoon.

The Crossing Bridge from
Pioneer Park looks tiny —
I have measured the
distance with my feet there and
back — three and a half hours.

Taking account of what an addict does
Watching the behavior and trying to
Understand why the addict doesn't have
A common sense of self-respect that

Should prevent the stupid indulgence of
Temporary pleasure — when the certain
Consequences are terrible and
It's easy to see the bitterness and

Remorse afterwards — it is confounding
To witness the continuation of
Addiction — as addiction inspires
The disgust and repulsion of people

Who used to be friends — and the family
Is exhausted with useless excuses.

Only another
addict who has
sobriety can put
the puzzle pieces
together.

The momentum of the downward spiral
Was baffling as the people who cared
Lacked the power to influence addiction
And I really had no explanation

Because the ecstasy of the drug had
Vanished and there was no longer any
Pleasure or escape in the addiction —
But I was willing to do anything

To turn my life around — and I did by
By listening to addicts who thought and
Felt and behaved like me — and I might not
Have done it if the situation had

Not arrived when the effective words were
Said with kindness to pierce my denial.

I did not know that
I was dying until
the desperation
was revealed to me
by other addicts.

Sadly Kit Cat is too clever for his
Own good and he is expert at waiting
For the few seconds when the door opens —
And when it was time to feed the cats at

Noon yesterday Johnnie and Henry were
Present but Kit was nowhere in the house
And I could only surmise that he went
Out when I did without me noticing

Because that's the only explanation —
And a downpour began in the morning
And a heavy rain continued during
The day and Kit Cat was nowhere to be

Found — so as clever as he is he chose
The absolutely worst day to escape.

I laid awake in bed
with memories of Kit Cat's
absurdities and
antics hoping he has the
common sense to return home.

It is unnatural to keep a cat
Within a house for a lifetime when a
Cat is intended to use the stalking
Waiting and pouncing skills it was born with

And Kit Cat is much like a miniature
Mountain lion who I would notice at the
Window everyday alertly watching
And listening outdoors — and so his urge

To escape is irrepressible and
Honorable and perhaps I'm being
Too possessive in my concern but I
Am worrying about where he is in

The rain whether he can elude the dogs
And will he be able to return home?

About 4 a.m.
a familiar utterance
came through the window —
I went out to meet Kit Cat
and he was completely dry.

Every Saturday throughout the year we
Gather for morning meditation — and
In between our sitting meditation
We stand up and leave the cozy chapel

Within the church and enter the roomy
Sanctuary where the stained glass windows
Filter the sunlight of the season — and
With a clear bell we begin walking in

A meditative fashion stepping and
Carefully attending to the rising
And placing of our feet and breathing in
With the rising and breathing out with the

Falling of every step harmonizing
Motion and letting our mind waves ripple.

There is a balance
of motion and thought —
attending to what
we do everyday
with a bit more care.

I am what I give my attention to
This morning and I am dwelling on a
Person who is not quite a friend and am
Considering the friction between us

That I believe is based on differing
Opinions and on a rivalry for
Dominance within a circle of friends —
And I hold my thoughts gently within the

Oval my hands are making as my hands
Are resting motionless on my lap as
I am meditating with my legs crossed
With my back straight — and I am giving my

Mind the freedom to show me the burdens
It has so I can let them dissipate.

I accept my
perceptions may be
an imagined
contrivance so
I hold them gently.

When holding my thoughts within the oval
I am making with my hands as I am
Meditating in the morning I am
Gentle with myself — and when money and

Bills come to mind I recognize fear and
Let it go — and when criticism of
People arises there is the urge to
Control that in time dissipates — and my

Hands do not become fists — and I do not
Grasp and fling my disturbance away — but
I am determinedly patient and hold
My thoughts gently letting my thoughts arise

And disappear because my thoughts are like
Smoke vanishing into a vast sky.

The crossing of my
legs and the discipline of
keeping my back straight
serve to position my mind
to reveal life's combustion.

When I am quiet and determined to
Sit for a length of time without moving
I am willing to let my thoughts arise
Without interference — and I may be

Angry with someone — or I may be so
Nervous about a situation which
I can't control — and it is really hard
To sit quietly and discover the

Depth of my emotion — but I resolved
To sit quietly for a length of time
And it is a worthy practice to let
The power of my emotions arise

So that I engage with the magnitude
And grow some moxie by facing the truth.

Energy builds
energy transforms
and alters
perceptions.

There is a quiet joy in learning how
To harmonize my energy — so that
I can encourage the activity
I love when I have the clarity of

Mind to do it — going to sleep early
Enough to wake early enough when
The neighborhood is quiet enough so
That I can enjoy the playing with thoughts

That my mind does enthusiastically
Is a method of starting the day that
Took almost sixty years to discover —
Without haste and distraction I wake up

And assume a meditative posture
And my thoughts will bloom into gentle hands.

When distraction and
haste overcomes me
occasionally
an underlying
quiet is present.

I know it is time to trim my nails when
One of them cracks and causes discomfort
When I am putting in or taking out
Something from my pocket — and because I

Am left handed I do a better job
Clipping the nails of my right hand and I
Can generate tremendous and skillful
Leverage filing down the sharp edges to

A pleasing smoothness — but when I apply
The clipper to my left fingers with my
Right hand it is a tricky endeavor
And I am never a slap dash person

But for my left hand I will make due with
A little less propitious result.

The little toe on
my left foot is
hard — I twist it
with my right hand — aim —
and clip.

My eyes are

insightful

my arms are

handy and

my legs are

footy.

Vietnam

The French occupied Indochina
A century before the Second World
War and during the war the Japanese
Invaded and the Vietnamese starved —

And the Viet Minh arose to expel
The invaders with guerrilla warfare —
And American agents provided
Arms and training and the Americans

Admired Vietnamese patriots
Because the Americans remembered
Their colonial history — after the
War the French returned to repossess their

Colony and the French leader De Gaulle
Demanded American compliance.

The French would help
America fight Communists
in Europe — if
America were neutral
in French Indochina.

Marxism offers equality and
Economic freedom as long as the
Individual surrenders private
Property and accepts the leadership

Of the Vanguard — and in the twentieth
Century the Communists had their chance
In the revolutions they began to
Impose their system — and in the twenty-

First century it is apparent there
Never was a more idealistic
Form of government that created as
Many corpses as the Communists did —

In the Black Book of Communism the
Low estimate is one hundred million.

Half the world was
frightened to death of
the Communist
revolutionaries who
were transforming nations.

An individual can embody
The contradictions the sympathies and
The inspiration of many people
And so when trying to understand the

Heroic essence of Ho Chi Minh who
Led the Vietnamese to expel the
French from Vietnam it is important
To take account of the motivation

He instilled in his people — was it his
Marxist ideology imported
From foreigners or a Vietnamese
Yearning to rid the country of foreign

Occupation that fired the hearts of
His people and compelled self-sacrifice?

The American
presidents and generals
said America
was saving Vietnam from
Communist domination.

Divine omniscience takes account of
History and culture and spirit but
Americans were scared of atom bombs
And Communist expansion throughout the

Earth and with the passage of time it is
Easy to see that the Vietnamese
Communists were never a threat to the
American homeland but presidents

Were compelled to oppose Marxism in
Proxy nations with limited warfare
Involving ambush and sabotage and
Calculated escalation always

With the prevention of atomic war
In mind with the Russians and the Chinese.

The presidents
Kennedy Johnson Nixon
were probably right —
reelection depended
on fighting Communism.

The American military aimed
To win the hearts and minds of the people
Of South Vietnam by supporting a
Series of corrupt and unpopular

Vietnamese leaders in Saigon — and
American soldiers conducted search
And destroy missions in South Vietnam
Confronting the Viet Cong and the North

Vietnamese Army — and marauding
Americans uprooted people and
Burned hamlets and rice — and Americans
Blundered into ambushes and booby

Traps in rice paddies and elephant grass
And in the sweltering hilly jungle.

Americans
encountered
passivity
during the day and
enemies at night.

The war in Vietnam coincided
With the evolution of civil rights
In America when Americans
Were struggling with the inequities

Between the blacks and people of lighter
Color and it became more apparent
As the war progressed that the blacks and the
Poor — the people who prospered the least — were

More likely to be drafted and wounded
And killed because they lacked the privileges
Of the wealthy — and it was obvious
That the South Vietnamese as the war

Dragged didn't like being uprooted and
Resented American foreigners.

The Vietnamese
were forced from the countryside
into city slums —
they saw the corruption of
profiteering generals.

Only after the passage of decades
When the people who made the decisions
Were safely dead were the memoranda
Of the presidents revealed in a

Documentary that demonstrates that
Kennedy and Johnson and Nixon and
The top advisors McNamara and
Kissinger from the beginning were

Aware that victory was doubtful but
They kept sending Americans soldiers
To assault another meaningless hill in
The jungle and when the hill was taken

The soldiers left it behind and they took
The bodies of their dead — in most cases.

The enemy died
at a rate of ten to one
American death
so victory was assured
General Westmoreland said.

The America people did not want
To believe that President Johnson and
General Westmoreland would ever be
Dishonest about the war but when the

Enemy suddenly assaulted so
Much South Vietnamese territory
On the morning of the Tet Offensive
It was revealed that the American

Strategy was not effective and that
The enemy was quite ferociously
Determined — and then the American
Public began to realize there was

A difference between what they were told
And what was happening in Vietnam.

Limited war in
Vietnam was becoming
ugly and senseless
and Americans perceived
their leaders were lying.

The war in Vietnam impacted on
American society like a
Hammer shattering a framed mirror — and
The frame keeps the shards from falling out — but

Ever since the war we see ourselves as
Divided factions quite suspicious of
Each other — when we separate into
Racial and ethnic and class rivalries —

And when we are confronted by hostile
Forces beyond our borders we argue
Whether we are the cause of the conflict
Whether we have a right to self-defense

Or whether on balance we are a good
Nation seeking for a proper response.

The Vietnam War
reminds Americans
sometimes politicians
are less than truthful and
vigilance is important.

It is fitting that the Vietnam War
Memorial is near America's
Capitol building and the White House and
Arlington Cemetery and it is

Very peaceful with shady trees and a
Gently sloping lawn — the memorial
Dispenses with the airs of triumph that
Often typify a nation's symbols —

It is a wall of black granite with the
Names of soldiers who died sacrificing
Themselves for the good of America
Inscribed in stone so that loved ones can reach

Out and touch the names of those they lost — and
Hopefully we will grow humility.

If war memorials
were required to inscribe
all the names of those
who die would we
have fewer wars?

Vietnam hints
perhaps we may not
comprehend everything
we think we know.

— *Tekkan*

www.ingramcontent.com/pod-product-compliance
Lightning Source LLC
Chambersburg PA
CBHW052104070526
44584CB00017B/2327